Chapters

Contents

Preface

*I*n 1989, I wrote my autobiography entitled *The Wanderer.* Afterward I received many comments from readers about how interesting my life was. Quite frankly, I've always believed that everyone has a fascinating story to tell, they just need to answer the right questions, and the context in which to do it.

In writing my book, questions were used as a framework not only to enable proper sequencing of events, but to facilitate easier recollection of thoughts and memories associated with these events. How often do we ask ourselves: "What are the important milestones in my life?", or "What did this person really mean to me?" Upon answering these questions, a certain clarity about priorities and order in my life emerged. I was able to see the "big picture."

This book, *Chapters,* emerged from this knowledge, and when I met Andi, we decided to begin the task of compiling questions, some fact based, some open-ended, to create an autobiography for every individual, a legacy to be passed down through generations.

Chapters will help you to step outside of yourself and become more objective about your past. In many ways the questions will help you get "unstuck" in your life; you'll be able to move forward and answer from long-held thoughts or dreams. At times it is important to know when to let go.

When you complete this book, it will contain who you are. If you choose to pass it on, you will have established an everlasting bond, that of sharing your thoughts, your hopes and dreams with those you love and who love you.

God Bless,
Dion DiMucci

Acknowledgments

We would like to thank the entire staff at Health Communications for their generous support and kind spirit. Special thanks go to Peter Vegso, Gary Seidler, Christine Belleris, Allison Janse, Kim Weiss, Ronni O'Brien and Randee Goldsmith.

Andi gratefully acknowledges: Molly Litt; A. Nicholas Masi, Ph.D.; Wendy Masi, Ph.D.; Pamela Jordan; Janice Bing; Cathy Henretta; Nomie Moss; and Marc, Sari and Leslie Wiener.

She dedicates this book to the memory of her father, Max E. Litt.

Dion gratefully acknowledges: Susan DiMucci; Ben Troxell; Bill Tuohy; Phillys Moffet; Ed Cayia; Sandy Scott; Davin Seay; Tane; Lark; August; and Andi (a big thanks).

Introduction

What busy lives we lead. Our days are filled with work and chores, then we go home to additional responsibilities. Even our recreational time is spent viewing other people's lives via television, movies and computer screens. When did you last think about life; the ups and downs, the memories and experiences that shaped the individual you are today?

A major void in our lives today is a lack of communication, not only with others, but with ourselves. There is a desperate need to get in touch with feelings, memories and thoughts, and in writing these thoughts comes realization, self-discovery and, most important, validation.

Everyone can write their own autobiography. Well, this is your chance. With pen in hand, take this journey that will thrill, surprise, inspire and reveal the genuinely unique person that you are.

Chapters has been subdivided into age categories, beginning with your earliest memories, and ending with your most recent. The questions are relevant to those specific time periods, and aid in providing continuity and cohesiveness to your answers, hopefully connecting the dots in your life. There are no right or wrong answers, no judgment or bias involved and, most important, no deadline. The only requirement is to be honest and uninhibited in your answers—for this is *your* story.

CHAPTER 1

The Nurturing Years
Birth to Six

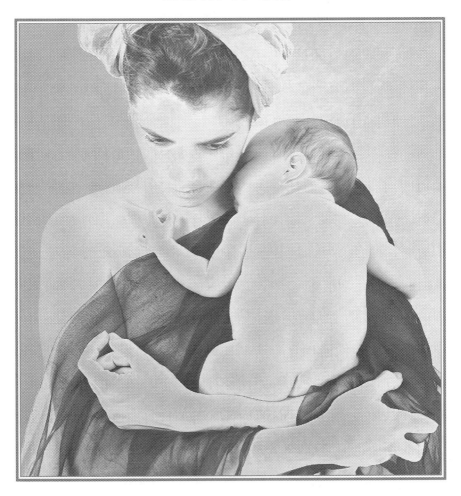

*Infancy conforms to nobody;
all conform to it.*

—EMERSON, *SELF-RELIANCE*

*T*his chapter will be the most challenging in terms of memory recall. It may be helpful to look at early pictures, or talk to parents or other family members to get more accurate information regarding historical facts, appearance, personality, etc.

Relax. Close your eyes and think back to a simpler time when a big decision was what toy to play with, or what stuffed animal to sleep with. Maybe you can remember playing in the sandbox at nursery school, or climbing a jungle gym; perhaps losing a tooth, and waking up to find money under your pillow, or crying and being comforted by Mom.

You will see how easily these memories flow from your mind when prompted. We all need to get in touch with the child within us.

1. What is your first memory?

2. Where were you born?

3. Who was president and what was happening politically at the time of your birth?

4. If adopted, describe how you were told and at what age. Did you feel special?

5. Did you live in the city, or in the country? In a house, or in an apartment? Describe your surroundings.

6. Describe what you looked like.

7. How do parents or other family members describe you as a child?

8. Describe your relationship with your mother.

9. Describe your relationship with your father.

10. Describe your relationship with your siblings.

11. What was your position in the sibling line? How did you feel about it?

12. Were you closer to your mother or father? Why?

13. Do you remember feeling loved as a child?

14. Do you remember a favorite adult (other than parents) whom you admired?

15. What were your favorite nursery rhymes?

16. What were your favorite radio and television shows, movies and performers?

17. What foods did you enjoy eating? Describe dinnertime at your house.

18. Did you have a favorite scent—for example, your mom's perfume or dad's cologne—or smell that you liked? Describe it.

19. Remember the games you played outside with friends and write about them.

20. What was your favorite game, and why?

21. Describe your favorite toy.

22. If you had a pet during this time, describe it. What other animals did you like?

23. Describe your first day of school.

24. What did you like about school?

25. What do you remember about your teachers?

26. Who was your favorite teacher, and why?

27. Describe what made you happy.

28. What made you sad?

29. What type of trouble did you get into?

30. What punishment do you remember receiving?

31. Write about an embarrassing event.

32. What did you want to be when you grew up?

33. What recreational activities did you like, (i.e., swimming, crafts, etc.), and why?

34. Describe classes you may have begun at this age, such as dance, karate or gymnastics.

35. What was bedtime like? Can you remember any stories read to you?

36. Did you have a favorite baby-sitter? Describe him or her.

37. Describe a special event you attended with adults, such as a circus, concert or a baseball game.

38. Describe your favorite family vacation.

Photos

Photos

Photos

CHAPTER 2

The Wonder Years

Seven to Eleven

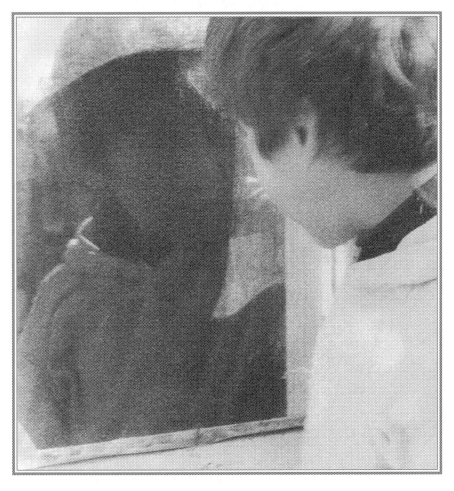

*Childhood is the kingdom
where nobody dies.*

—EDNA ST. VINCENT MILLAY

With first grade under your belt, you took your first steps toward independence. There were anxieties about school and separation from parents, but let us not forget that first crush on your teacher or schoolmate.

You may remember learning how to ride a bicycle, or playing outside with neighborhood friends. With the loss of additional teeth and the first of many growth spurts, this period marked the beginning of an "awkward stage," as prepubescent hormones began to rise. However, you gained more mobility and freedom as you rode your bicycle through the neighborhood and to school, while transporting friends on the handlebars, or in tow on the back.

1. Where did you live? Describe your neighborhood.

2. What did you look like?

3. How was your relationship with your parents?

4. How did you get along with your siblings?

5. Describe your mother and father's physical characteristics as well as their personalities.

6. Describe your room. Did you share it with anyone?

7. Describe first grade.

8. What did you learn in school?

9. What subjects did you most enjoy?

10. Did you have a special teacher who influenced you? How?

11. Describe your school lunches.

12. Who were your best friends? What did they look like, and what did you do with them?

13. Describe your pets. Did you take care of them?

14. Describe your stuffed animal collection. Did you have a favorite doll?

15. Describe your trips to visit relatives.

16. What did you learn from your grandparents?

17. What one person during this time had the most profound effect on you? Why?

18. Describe the day you learned how to ride a bicycle. Who taught you to ride?

19. What activities did you enjoy doing?

20. What sports did you participate in?

21. What were your least favorite activities?

22. What made you most happy?

23. What was the funniest thing that happened to you?

24. Describe your favorite birthday party. Do you remember any special gifts?

25. Who were your role models?

26. Who was your favorite superhero (cartoon, comic strip or magazine)? Why?

27. What was your favorite color, and why?

28. Write about dinnertime. Did you have meals together as a family?

29. What were your favorite and least favorite dishes?

30. What was the most memorable thing that happened to you during this time?

31. Did you play any musical instruments? If so, did you enjoy performing? What were your practice sessions like?

32. What occupied most of your time, and what were you thinking about most often?

33. Write about a relationship that was meaningful to you at this time.

34. Did you ever think about God? What type of religious worship did you follow?

35. How did you relate to the opposite sex during this time?

36. Do you remember your nightmares? Any recurring ones?

37. What were your fears?

38. What was the most unfair thing that happened to you during these years?

39. Did you ever lie? If so, were you ever caught lying? How did that make you feel?

40. If you could change your actions during these years, what would you change?

41. Looking back on these years, did life seem simpler, or more complicated than it does now?

Photos

Photos

CHAPTER 3

The Impressionable Years
Twelve to Fourteen

*Youth even in its sorrows, always
has a brilliancy of its own.*

—VICTOR HUGO, *LES MISERABLES*

READER/CUSTOMER CARE SURVEY

If you are enjoying this book, please help us serve you better and meet your changing needs by taking a few minutes to complete this survey. Please fold it & drop it in the mail.

Name: _____

Address: _____

_____

Tel. # _____

As a special **"Thank You"** we'll send you exciting news about interesting books and a valuable Gift Certificate.
It's Our Pleasure to Serve You!

(1) Gender: 1) ____ Female 2) ____ Male

(2) Age: 1)___ 18-25 4)___ 46-55
2)___ 26-35 5)___ 56-65
3)___ 36-45 6)___ 65+

(3) Marital status:

1)___ Married 3)___ Single 5)___ Widowed
2)___ Divorced 4)___ Partner

(4) Is this book: 1)___ Purchased for self?
2)___ Purchased for others?
3)___ Received as gift?

(5) How did you find out about this book?

1)___ Catalog 2)___ Store Display
Newspaper
3)___ Best Seller List
4)___ Article/Book Review
5)___ Advertisement
Magazine
6)___ Feature Article
7)___ Book Review
8)___ Advertisement
9)___ Word of Mouth
A)___ T.V./Talk Show (Specify) _____
B)___ Radio/Talk Show (Specify) _____
C)___ Professional Referral _____
D)___ Other (Specify) _____

Which Health Communications book are you currently reading? _____

(6) What subject areas do you enjoy reading most? (Rank in order of enjoyment)

1)___ Women's Issues/   5)___ New Age/
Relationships   Altern. Healing
2)___ Business Self Help 6)___ Aging
3)___ Soul/Spirituality/ 7)___ Parenting
Inspiration   8)___ Diet/Nutrition/
4)___ Recovery   Exercise/Health

(14) What do you look for when choosing a personal growth book?

(Rank in order of importance)
1)___ Subject   3)___ Author
2)___ Title   4)___ Price
Cover Design   5)___ In Store Location

(19) When do you buy books?

(Rank in order of importance)
1)___ Christmas
2)___ Valentine's Day
3)___ Birthday
4)___ Mother's Day
5)___ Other (Specify _____

(23) Where do you buy your books?

(Rank in order of frequency of purchases)
1)___ Bookstore   6)___ Gift Store
2)___ Price Club   7)___ Book Club
3)___ Department Store 8)___ Mail Order
4)___ Supermarket/   9)___ T.V. Shopping
Drug Store   A)___ Airport
5)___ Health Food Store

Additional comments you would like to make to help us serve you better.

_____

_____

Thank You !!

*T*his chapter is aptly named, for it was a period fraught with adolescent angst as the hormones kicked into high gear. It was an awkward and a sensitive stage filled with pimples and self-doubt as you transitioned from childhood into adulthood.

These years clearly marked the teenager's reaction to authority, for daughters saw their mothers as adversaries, while boys became more rebellious and defiant. However tumultuous, these were some of the best years, packed with flourishing friendships, increased self-reliance, and a sexual energy that emerged from the physical and emotional changes that took place.

1. Where did you live? Describe the neighborhood.

2. Describe your bedroom.

3. How was your relationship with your parents? How about your siblings?

4. If you were an only child, describe how that felt.

5. How was your parents' relationship? If they divorced, how did you handle it?

6. How did you change physically at this time? Describe how you felt about that.

7. Did you share these feelings with anyone?

8. What did you study in school?

9. Were you a good student?

10. Describe your study habits.

11. What subject did you most enjoy? What subject did you dislike?

12. Did you have a special teacher who influenced you? How?

13. How much time did you spend on the telephone? Who did you talk to and what did you talk about?

14. What time did you go to bed and what would you do to unwind?

15. Were you an extrovert or an introvert? Did you need to be with a group, or were you more of a loner?

16. Recall a memory of disobedience, either in school or at home.

17. What were your best qualities at this time?

18. What gave you a sense of security? Explain why.

19. Did you enjoy performing for people? What were your talents?

20. Were you athletic? What did you compete in?

21. Were you a good sport, or a sore loser? Recall your feelings when you won or lost a game.

22. Was humor an important part of your life? How did humor get you through a difficult situation?

23. Describe an experience involving discrimination that you either witnessed, or were a victim of.

24. Can you ever remember feeling truly surprised? What was the reason?

25. What was the most frightening thing that happened to you during this time?

26. Did you ever have a paranormal (clairvoyant or déjà vu) experience?

27. Could you speak another language? If so, which language and why did you choose to study it?

28. Were you generally healthy, or do you remember getting sick often?

29. Did you ever have a broken arm or leg? How did it happen and how did you feel? Did your friends give you special attention because of it?

30. How were your eating habits during these years?

31. What were your friends like?

32. Did you ever have any conflicts with them? How did you resolve those conflicts?

33. What kinds of parties did you go to, and what did you do there?

34. What were your feelings about sex during this time?

35. Did your parents openly discuss sex with you or not?

36. Did your parents discuss drugs with you? How did they approach this subject?

37. Were you introduced to cigarettes, alcohol, or any other controlled or illegal substance?

38. If so, how did you handle the peer pressure regarding these things?

39. Did you have a sexual experience at this time? If so, how did you handle it?

40. Did you ever feel "different" than other kids? If so, how?

41. Did other kids ever exclude you from the group? How?

42. Do you remember the death of someone special to you? Explain how you felt.

43. Did you think of your family as rich or poor? Explain how you felt about this.

Photos

Photos

CHAPTER 4

The Breakaway Years

Fifteen to Eighteen

No legacy is so rich as honesty.

—WILLIAM SHAKESPEARE

The Breakaway Years greatly signified a rite of passage for most teenagers. Aside from raging hormones, obtaining a driver's license was prominent. There were also "make out" parties, possible experimentation with illegal substances, and hanging out with friends.

You may recall feeling consumed by a love relationship, or by school work and extracurricular activities. Popularity and being part of a group was critical during this time, but equally important was the shift in focus to a course of study that would eventually lead you to that final release of parental control: graduation from high school, and living away from home either at college, or on your own.

1. Where did you live? Describe your neighborhood.

2. What did you look like?

3. Describe your relationship with your parents and siblings.

4. What did you study in school?

5. What subjects did you most enjoy?

6. Did you have a special teacher who influenced you? How?

7. Did you have a girlfriend or boyfriend? If so, what made her or him special?

8. What did you do on dates?

9. Did you attend any school dances such as the Sadie Hawkins Day dance, homecoming, temple or church dances? If so, describe your experiences there.

10. Were you popular in school? What clubs or committees did you belong to? If you were a class officer, describe what that was like.

11. Did you participate in any extracurricular activities, such as sports, cheerleading, drama, chorus or band? Describe how you felt when you did these things.

12. What did you do after school and on weekends?

13. Did you have a job? If so, describe it and what you did with the money you earned.

14. What was your daily routine?

15. What goals had you set in your life at this time?

16. Describe the dreams you had.

17. Describe your favorite place to be and why.

18. What was your favorite way to spend time?

19. What was the best thing that happened to you during this period?

20. What was the worst?

21. Write about your hobbies and how you felt during these activities.

22. What did you aspire to be when you grew up?

23. What relative (other than parents) was special to you? Why?

24. What books affected you and what were the reasons?

25. What movies, actors or other performers had an impact on your life? Why?

26. What different ways did you use your imagination?

27. What games did you play (solitary and in groups)?

28. Describe your best friend.

29. Did you ever experience jealousy over a friend or sibling? Describe what provoked these feelings and how you handled the relationship.

30. Who were your teenage idols in movies, music and sports?

31. What types of music were you interested in?

32. Was worship part of your family's routine? If yes, describe its meaning to you.

33. What was your favorite holiday? Describe the celebration.

34. Remember the physical changes that took place while going through puberty and adolescence. Write about this time.

35. Describe your first kiss and your first sexual encounter.

36. Were you aware of birth control methods? Which did you use, if any?

37. Can you recall some fun sleepovers with friends or family?

38. Did you take any memorable vacations?

39. Who taught you how to drive a car?

40. Describe the day you received your driver's license.

41. What kind of car did you drive? Did you have any car accidents?

42. How did your parents feel about your driving?

43. Did you ever feel indestructible? Describe those feelings.

44. Did you ever engage in self-destructive behavior? If so, what?

45. Did you go to the senior prom? Describe your date and the entire evening.

46. What were your feelings the last day of school?

47. Did you look forward to leaving home? Why?

48. Describe your graduation.

Photos

Photos

Photos

CHAPTER 5

The Social Years
Nineteen to Twenty-five

Life is the Art.

—Unknown

This chapter contains some monumental events, such as leaving home for the first time, attending college, turning twenty-one, living in dorms with roommates, or living alone in an apartment working towards a career. Perhaps you met the love of your life, got married and settled down with children.

Although the title reflects the "social" aspect of this time, a significant amount of intellectual growth and emotional maturity took place, too. Major decisions, such as where you were going to live and what job you were going to take had to be made, and these choices ultimately impacted your future.

1. Where did you live? Describe your neighborhood.

2. What did you look like?

3. What did you like or dislike about how you looked?

4. Did you ever consider changing or did you actually alter your looks with plastic surgery at this time?

5. How was your relationship with your parents and siblings?

6. How did you relate to authority figures?

7. How did you spend the summer after graduation?

8. What college did you attend and how did you choose it?

9. How did you feel when your parents dropped you off at school?

10. Describe the campus, your living quarters and your room-mate.

11. Did you declare a major? If so, what was it, and why did you choose it?

12. Were there any professors who you would categorize as mentors?

13. If you did not go to college, where did you work?

14. Did this work ultimately lead you to a career?

15. What was your starting salary?

16. What were your fears during these years?

17. What made you most happy during this time?

18. What made you most angry?

19. Who were your friends at this time?

20. Write about a time when you pulled an all-nighter.

21. How did turning twenty-one affect you?

22. How did you celebrate this birthday?

23. What made you laugh?

24. Describe your daydreams.

25. Did you have a talent that you stifled, or had you begun to nurture it?

26. Describe the kind of support you received from family and friends.

27. What song or poem had great meaning for you? Explain why.

28. What was the best concert you ever attended? Describe the event.

29. Did you have a camping experience, or an outside adventure you can write about?

30. What types of people were you attracted to?

31. What attributes specifically drew you to them?

32. Were you involved in an ongoing relationship? If so, describe the feelings you had for your mate.

33. What were your feelings about marriage and children?

34. Did you smoke or take drugs?

35. Did you ever have a bad experience with drugs? If so, describe it.

36. What were the repercussions of this experience?

37. Who was president and what was the political climate during this time?

38. Was the country at war? If so, describe how you were affected by the conflict.

39. What threatened you most at this time in your life?

40. Did you or someone you know serve in a war? How did this affect you?

41. If there was a war to which you were opposed, would you still fight for your country?

42. Can you remember a national crisis (i.e., World War II or JFK's assassination)? Describe where you were, and how this historical turning point affected you.

43. Can you recall a heroic event in which you were involved or witnessed?

44. When did you first realize you were not a kid anymore?

45. Were you a collector? What did you collect?

46. Remember a gift you treasured and write about it.

Photos

Photos

Photos

CHAPTER 6

The Serious Years

Twenty-six to Thirty-nine

*Do not follow where the path may lead.
Go instead where there is no path
and leave a trail.*

—AUTHOR UNKNOWN

*W*hen we think of these years, the word commitment comes to mind. We may have embarked on a career or on a marriage and family. Commitment to a job or to a spouse and children was most likely crucial to achieving success.

These serious years reflected a defining moment in our lives, one in which we developed an appreciation for life, for priorities, and a sense of ourselves. We came into our own and began to enjoy the fruits of our labors as we acquired material things to enhance our surroundings, make life easier and entertain us.

This was a time when hard work and dedication began to pay off, and what was of major importance was gaining respect from our superiors and coworkers, as well as respect from our friends and loved ones.

1. Where did you live? Describe your neighborhood.

2. What did you look like?

3. How was your relationship with your parents and siblings?

4. What type of work were you doing?

5. Did you find your work satisfying?

6. Describe your coworkers.

7. In regard to your career, who most influenced you and how did they help direct you to your goal?

8. If married, how did you meet your spouse? Describe your first date.

9. Write about prenuptial preparations (include shower, engagement and bachelor/bachlorette parties).

10. If single, describe your feelings about being unattached.

11. Describe some of your more memorable dates—good and bad.

12. What were your feelings on the institution of marriage?

13. Did spirituality and faith play an important part in your life?

14. What were your beliefs in a hereafter?

15. If you had to live either one day or one year of your life over, which one would it be and why?

16. What was the best day of your life?

17. What was the worst?

18. What did you learn from your parents and/or grandparents?

19. What kind of people were you intolerant of?

20. Which of your parents' personality traits did you see in yourself?

21. What was the greatest obstacle in your life?

22. What kind of relationship did you have with your neighbors?

23. Write about the pets you owned and what they meant to you.

24. If you have children, describe how you found out you were going to be a parent.

25. How did prospective parenthood affect your spouse and other family members?

26. Describe your pregnancy and the delivery of your children.

27. Did you experience depression during this time? Write about your moods surrounding the birth of your babies.

28. What changes occurred in your life with the addition of children?

29. Did you ever feel lost, confused or extremely depressed? Describe your feelings and your recovery.

30. What one person (living or deceased) would you have liked to have met and why?

31. If you had three wishes, what would they be and why?

32. Can you remember being moved by a speaker during a live forum? Who was it and how were you influenced by that person?

33. Reveal a secret dream you had.

34. Describe the first time you were affected by:

Death

Money

Love

God

Photos

Photos

Photos

CHAPTER 7

The Midlife Years
Forty to Fifty-five

*It's not what you do that determines
who you are; it's who you are that
determines what you do.*

—DION DIMUCCI

he midlife years were profound in the sense that along with responsibilities, children, work and relationship demands, you were now confronted with your own mortality. Many at this time are sandwiched in between caregiving to their children as well as caregiving to their parents.

Yet these years were rewarding because, as you accomplished certain goals, you also began to pursue new interests and hobbies with an invigorated enthusiasm. You were able to look back and reflect on the past, while looking forward to the future with a knowledge and wisdom you did not possess twenty years before.

Self-help was key during this time. While we strived to better our minds and bodies with anti-aging remedies, we felt stronger in our convictions and quicker in our resolve.

1. Where did you live? Describe your surroundings.

2. What did you look like?

3. Describe your relationship with your spouse or partner.

4. How was your relationship with your children?

5. Describe your relationship with your siblings.

6. What kind of relationship did you have with your in-laws?

7. Were you working? Describe your job.

8. If you were involved with volunteer work, describe it.

9. What did your social life consist of?

10. Did you enjoy eating at home or out?

11. Write about the worst meal you ever had.

12. What event(s) stood out during these years?

13. What were your worries and concerns?

14. If you could live in another country, where would it be and why?

15. How did turning forty affect you?

16. How did turning fifty affect you?

17. Did you attend any high school reunions? Describe the event and how it felt to see childhood friends and sweethearts.

18. Were you ever given a surprise party? Describe it and how you felt.

19. Did you ever give a surprise party for someone else? Write about that experience.

20. How did you feel when you developed your first wrinkle or sprouted your first gray hair?

21. Did you ever have plastic surgery? If so, describe the procedure and how you felt afterward.

22. Describe your health at this time. How physically active were you?

23. Did acquiring more material things make you happier at this time of your life? Explain.

24. Write about your really good friends during these years.

25. How did your relationship with your parents change during these years?

26. How did you feel about watching your parents grow older?

27. If your parents are deceased, describe your feelings and experiences surrounding their death. How did their passing affect your relationship with your siblings?

28. If you have children, describe yourself as a parent.

29. Are you a grandparent? If so, how was that role different from being a parent?

30. If you were president of the United States, what would be the most important problem you would address and what would be your solution?

31. Have you made a contribution of either time or money to philanthropic causes? What were they and how did you become involved?

32. Did you ever help out a person in need on the spur of the moment? Describe the situation and how you felt afterward.

33. Have you ever found something valuable? Describe the outcome of this find.

34. What events did you most enjoy?

35. What musical instruments do you still play? What lessons did you begin at this stage of your life?

36. Give an account of the perfect life.

37. Describe the most romantic evening you had during these years.

38. Had you ever entertained thoughts of infidelity?

39. How have you dealt with temptation and indiscretion?

40. Did you endure any traumatic events during this time?

41. If you had the opportunity to give one piece of advice to a large group of people, what would it be and why?

42. What was the best advice you received and from whom?

43. At this stage in your life, did you deny any of your unhealthy behaviors? Describe them and whether you found it difficult to change.

Photos

Photos

Photos

---- CHAPTER 8 ----

The Reassessment Years
Fifty-six to Sixty-five

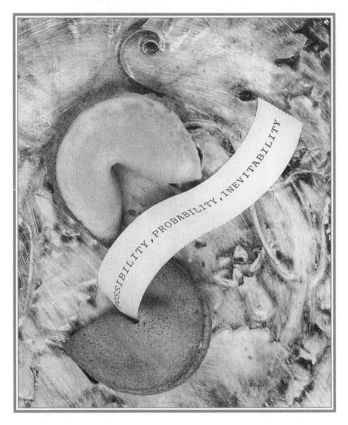

POSSIBILITY, PROBABILITY, INEVITABILITY

Life is a one-way street. No matter how many detours you take, none of them leads back. And once you know and accept that, life becomes much simpler.

—ISABEL MOORE

The questions in these last two chapters are more open-ended and philosophical. This is primarily because as people age, they become more introspective and reflective about their lives and their past.

This is a time when the need to resolve issues concerning children, grandchildren, marriage and career becomes paramount. It is also a time to prepare for the future both financially and emotionally, so as not to burden your loved ones later in life.

As you answer these questions, you may find that what is really important becomes realized, and the process of simplifying your life has begun.

1. Where did you live?

2. What did you look like?

3. How was your relationship with your children?

4. If you are a grandparent, describe your relationship with your grandchildren.

5. Write about your marital status, and the relationship with your significant other.

6. What did you enjoy doing together?

7. Did you enjoy sex more or less than when you were younger? Explain why.

8. Did you enjoy being alone or did you prefer socializing with others?

9. How did you relate to your age?

10. Did others treat you differently?

11. Describe your health. What was your exercise routine and your eating habits?

12. What other methods did you use to reduce stress?

13. What still interested you about life at this stage?

14. At this point in your life, did you feel contentment or frustration? Why?

15. What thoughts occupied your mind?

16. Write about a significant event that occurred during these years.

17. What does the term "senior citizen" mean to you?

18. Did you use your status to get discounts at various places?

19. If you have grandchildren, how did you spend time with them? How did it feel being a grandparent?

20. Describe your perfect day.

21. Is there any place you would like to visit? Why?

22. Describe the best vacation you ever took.

23. What brought you the most joy in your life?

24. In an age of uncertainty, what remained most constant in your life?

25. Was there a painting you admired? Describe it and what you felt when you gazed upon it.

26. Did you have fears of growing old? Describe those fears.

27. What were your feelings about society in general? Were things better or worse than when you were in your twenties and thirties?

28. How did you feel about the technological revolution, including the advent of the "computer age."

29. Did you spend more time reading or watching television than you used to? What should you have been spending more time doing instead?

30. What were your feelings about death?

31. What steps had you taken in preparation for your own funeral and burial?

32. What were your feelings regarding past lives? Did you believe that you had lived in another time and place?

33. What sacrifices have you made over the years. Were they worth it?

34. At what age in life did you feel your best physically, emotionally and psychologically?

35. If you were banished to a remote island and were able to take six people with you, who would they be and why?

36. If you could make a movie based on your life, would it be categorized as a comedy, drama, suspense, adventure or horror story? Describe this film.

37. Were there any issues that needed resolution at this time?

Photos

Photos

Photos

CHAPTER 9

The Reaffirming Years
Sixty-six and Beyond

*Old age is a second childhood in which
earliest memories revive.*

—CAMILLE PAGLIA, *SEXUAL PERSONAE*

With the completion of this chapter, you will have an autobiography that you can treasure alone or share, as your family members pass your legacy on to future generations.

In writing this last chapter you should feel a great sense of satisfaction, for history has now been recorded, but not carved in stone. You may want to return to a question or chapter at some later time, and add a thought or rewrite an answer. As we continue to evolve, so do our minds and ideas.

Who you are is a culmination of what you think, what you know, and what you have done. In a society so infatuated with youth and beauty, the wisdom, knowledge and courage that shines through the eyes of the aged is to be revered, and above all else, serve as a lasting memorial to the children of the world.

1. Where are you living?

2. What do you look like?

3. Describe your health, including surgeries you have had and the rehabilitation involved.

4. Has your relationship with your siblings been rewarding? If so, how?

5. Do you have any contentious family relationships? Describe your falling out.

6. What was your greatest loss?

7. Have you been able to cope with reversals in your financial life?

8. Have world problems ever affected your sleeping habits? How?

9. If you had six months to live, what would you set out to accomplish? Would you tell people?

10. Are you enjoying your retirement years?

11. Do you enjoy volunteer work? What kind of work do you do?

12. Have you kept in touch with any people you knew forty or more years ago?

13. Has it been difficult dealing with your failing hearing and
eyesight?

14. Do you ever get annoyed with any or all of your friends?
How so?

15. Have you had any memory lapses? Describe how that feels.

16. What about dealing with friends or siblings who have these problems?

17. What do you think is most important in life: health, wealth or friends? Explain why.

18. If you moved many times, how did it affect your ability to deal with people?

19. Do you find entering a room of perfect strangers a frightening or exhilarating experience?

20. Which contemporary politicians do you admire?

21. Do you feel that how you voted really mattered? Why?

22. Do you believe in religious scriptures, (i.e., the Bible, Torah or Koran)? How do you worship?

23. If you lost your spouse, how did you deal with it?

24. If you lost a child, how did you deal with it?

25. Have you ever contemplated suicide? What were the circumstances?

26. What are your feelings on aging, sickness and ultimately dying?

27. Would you consider having a relationship with a person you are not married to? Would you remain committed despite whatever problems arose?

28. What are your feelings about hospitals? Why?

29. What kinds of activities have you enjoyed during this part
of your life?

30. Do you feel secure?

31. Do you relate well with and enjoy being with young people?

32. For the most part, are you a loner or a person who likes to socialize? Has this characteristic changed over time?

33. Has age increased or decreased your patience? Explain why.

34. Have you remained sexually active or not? How do you feel about that?

35. How would you write your eulogy and epitaph?

Photos

Photos

Photos

About the Authors

_D_ion DiMucci is a rock 'n' roll original—New York City's very own singer of Bronx soul. He is best known for his hit songs: "The Wanderer," "Runaround Sue," "Teenager in Love," and "Abraham, Martin and John."

Dion was inducted into the Rock 'n' Roll Hall of Fame in 1989.

When not performing, he resides in South Florida with his wife, Susan, and his three daughters.

Andi Litt Wiener was born in Trenton, New Jersey, and has degrees in both psychology and music. She has worked with physically challenged individuals in Washington, D.C., and has been employed for the last eleven years in a sports medicine facility. She currently resides in South Florida with her husband, Marc, an architect, and daughters Sari and Leslie.

About the Photographer

Lissie Habie is an internationally renowned photographer who provided the beautiful artwork in this book. She resides in South Florida with her husband, Mitchell, and daughters Jessica and Jamie.

Books For Everyone

A 5th Portion of Chicken Soup for the Soul®

Whether readers are devotees of the series or first-time samplers, they will find this latest serving both riveting and heart-warming. This treasury is a tribute to life and humanity, with topics ranging the emotional and experiential gamut. The nature of the stories invites readers to enjoy *Chicken Soup* in whatever way they find most comforting—by the spoonful, by the bowl, or the whole soup pot in one sitting.
Code 5432..........$12.95

Chicken Soup for the Pet Lover's Soul

Like the bestselling *Chicken Soup for the Soul* books, animals bring out the goodness, humanity and optimism in people and speak directly to our souls. This joyous, inspiring and entertaining collection relates the unique bonds between animals and the people whose lives they've changed. Packed with celebrity pet-lore — this book relates the unconditional love, loyalty, courage and companionship that only animals possess.
Code 5718..........$12.95

Chicken Soup for the Mother's Soul

We can all remember a time when we were young and under the weather, and Mom soothed and nurtured us back to health with her magical chicken soup elixir. Now we can revisit those cherished moments with a delightful new batch of stories for and about mothers.
Code 4606........ $12.95

Chicken Soup for the Teenage Soul

This batch consists of 101 stories every teen can relate to and learn from—without feeling criticized or judged. You'll find lessons on the nature of friendship and love, the importance of belief in the future, the value of respect for oneself and others and much, much more.
Code 4630................$12.95

Available at your favorite bookstore or call 1-800-441-5569 for Visa or MasterCard orders. Prices do not include shipping and handling. Your response code is BKS.

Books to Nurture Your Body & Soul!

More from the
Chicken Soup for the Soul® Series

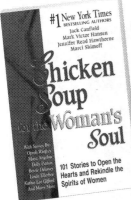

Chicken Soup for the Woman's Soul

The #1 *New York Times* bestseller guaranteed to inspire women with wisdom and insights that are uniquely feminine and always from the heart.
#4150—$12.95

Chicken Soup for the Christian Soul

Chicken Soup for the Christian Soul is an inspiring reminder that we are never alone or without hope, no matter how challenging or difficult our life may seem. In God we find hope, healing, comfort and love.
#5017—$12.95

Chicken Soup for the Soul® Series

Each one of these inspiring *New York Times* bestsellers brings you exceptional stories, tales and verses guaranteed to lift your spirits, soothe your soul and warm your heart! A perfect gift for anyone you love, including yourself!

A 4th Course of Chicken Soup for the Soul, #4592—$12.95
A 3rd Serving of Chicken Soup for the Soul, #3790—$12.95
A 2nd Helping of Chicken Soup for the Soul, #3316—$12.95
Chicken Soup for the Soul, #262X—$12.95

Selected books are also available in hardcover, large print, audiocassette and compact disc.

Available in bookstores everywhere or call **1-800-441-5569** for Visa or MasterCard orders.
Prices do not include shipping and handling. Your response code is **BKS**.